W9-CIK-848

CONTENTS

N. T. WRIGHT
FOR EVERYONE
BIBLE STUDY GUIDES

ROMANS

18 STUDIES FOR INDIVIDUALS AND GROUPS

N. T. WRIGHT

WITH PATTY PELL

IVP Connect

An imprint of InterVarsity Press
Downers Grove, Illinois

InterVarsity Press
P.O. Box 1400, Downers Grove, IL 60515-1426
World Wide Web: www.ivpress.com
E-mail: email@ivpress.com

InterVarsity Press® is the book-publishing division of InterVarsity Christian Fellowship/USA®, a
movement of students and faculty active on campus at hundreds of universities, colleges and schools
of nursing in the United States of America, and a member movement of the International Fellowship of
Evangelical Students. For information about local and regional activities, write Public Relations Dept.,
InterVarsity Christian Fellowship/USA, 6400 Schroeder Rd., P.O. Box 7895, Madison, WI 53707-7895, or
visit the IVCF website at <www.intervarsity.org>.

Cover design: Cindy Kiple
Cover image: Ashley Franklin/Trevillion Images

ISBN 978-0-8308-2186-0

Printed in the United States of America ∞

 InterVarsity Press is committed to protecting the environment and to the responsible use of
natural resources. As a member of Green Press Initiative we use recycled paper whenever
possible. To learn more about the Green Press Initiative, visit <www.greenpressinitiative.org>.

P   18   17   16   15   14   13   12   11   10   9   8   7   6   5   4   3   2

Y   24   23   22   21   20   19   18   17   16   15   14   13   12   11   10

GETTING THE MOST
OUT OF ROMANS

From time to time, scientists have sent space probes to Mars. The object of the exercise is, of course, to try to find out more about the planet which, although it's our nearest neighbor, is still over a hundred million miles away. For centuries people have imagined that there might be life on Mars, perhaps intelligent life. There are undoubtedly many new things to be learned, to be discovered. If only we could get there safely and work out what was going on.

A lot of people feel like that about Paul in general, and Romans in particular. Most people who have at least a nodding acquaintance with the Christian faith are aware that Paul was a striking and important figure in its early days. Many know that Romans is his greatest letter. Some may even have heard of the powerful effect this letter has had, over and over again, in the history of the church: great figures like Augustine, Luther and Karl Barth have studied it and come back with a fresh and challenging word from God. But, to many Christians in the Western world, Romans remains as much of a mystery as Mars. "I tried to read it once," they say, like a scientist describing yet another failed space probe, "but I got bogged down and I couldn't work it out."

A different problem lies in wait for those who have learned the Christian faith in the Western world. Many traditional Roman Catholics, and others in similar traditions, know that the Protestants have made Paul a great hero and are therefore suspicious of him. But there are problems for Protestants too.

Ever since the Reformation in the sixteenth century, many churches have taken Paul as their main guide, and have seen Romans as the book, above all, in which he sets out the basic doctrines they hold. Since part of my own background is firmly in this tradition—which is why I began studying this letter intensively for myself thirty years ago—I understand the power and importance of this tradition. But I have to report that it has only colonized certain parts of the great planet called Romans. It has mapped and discussed many craters, has analyzed many substances found in them, and has laid down well-trodden roads across some of the planet's surface. But there are other parts which have remained a mystery—not the least the parts about the coming together of Jews and Gentiles, which Paul comes back to again and again throughout the letter.

It is time for some new mapping, for paths to be hacked through unexplored territory. (For more on this letter, also see my *Paul for Everyone: Romans, Part One* and *Paul for Everyone: Romans, Part Two,* on which this guide is based, published by SPCK and Westminster John Knox.) We still need the old maps and roads, of course. We won't lose anything that they gave us. In fact, we shall find that we get more out of them by seeing and using them within Paul's own larger picture, of God, Jesus, the world and ourselves.

As we work through Romans in this guide (prepared with the help of Patty Pell, for which I am grateful), we may sometimes feel we are being swept along in a small boat on a swirling, bubbling river. We need to hold on tight if we're going to stay on board. But if we do, the energy and excitement of it all is unbeatable. The reason is obvious: because Romans is all about the God who, as Paul says, unveils his power and grace through the good news about Jesus. And, as Paul insists again and again, this power and grace is available for everyone who believes.

SUGGESTIONS FOR INDIVIDUAL STUDY

1. As you begin each study, pray that God will speak to you through his Word.

2. Read the introduction to the study and respond to the "Open" question that follows it. This is designed to help you get into the theme of the study.

3. Read and reread the Bible passage to be studied. Each study is designed to

help you consider the meaning of the passage in its context. The commentary and questions in this guide are based on my own translation of each passage found in the companion volume to this guide in the For Everyone series on the New Testament (published by SPCK and Westminster John Knox).

4. Write your answers to the questions in the spaces provided or in a personal journal. Each study includes three types of questions: observation questions, which ask about the basic facts in the passage; interpretation questions, which delve into the meaning of the passage; and application questions, which help you discover the implications of the text for growing in Christ. Writing out your responses can bring clarity and deeper understanding of yourself and of God's Word.

5. Each session features selected comments from the For Everyone series. These notes provide further biblical and cultural background and contextual information. They are designed not to answer the questions for you but to help you along as you study the Bible for yourself. For even more reflections on each passage, you may wish to have on hand a copy of the companion volume from the For Everyone series as you work through this study guide.

6. Use the guidelines in the "Pray" section to focus on God, thanking him for what you have learned and praying about the applications that have come to mind.

SUGGESTIONS FOR GROUP MEMBERS

1. Come to the study prepared. Follow the suggestions for individual study mentioned above. You will find that careful preparation will greatly enrich your time spent in group discussion.

2. Be willing to participate in the discussion. The leader of your group will not be lecturing. Instead, she or he will be asking the questions found in this guide and encouraging the members of the group to discuss what they have learned.

3. Stick to the topic being discussed. These studies focus on a particular pas-

sage of Scripture. Only rarely should you refer to other portions of the Bible or outside sources. This allows for everyone to participate on equal ground and for in-depth study.

4. Be sensitive to the other members of the group. Listen attentively when they describe what they have learned. You may be surprised by their insights! Each question assumes a variety of answers. Many questions do not have "right" answers, particularly questions that aim at meaning or application. Instead the questions push us to explore the passage more thoroughly.

   When possible, link what you say to the comments of others. Also, be affirming whenever you can. This will encourage some of the more hesitant members of the group to participate.

5. Be careful not to dominate the discussion. We are sometimes so eager to express our thoughts that we leave too little opportunity for others to respond. By all means participate! But allow others to also.

6. Expect God to teach you through the passage being discussed and through the other members of the group. Pray that you will have an enjoyable and profitable time together, but also that as a result of the study you will find ways that you can take action individually and/or as a group.

7. It will be helpful for groups to follow a few basic guidelines. These guidelines, which you may wish to adapt to your situation, should be read at the beginning of the first session.

   • Anything said in the group is considered confidential and will not be discussed outside the group unless specific permission is given to do so.

   • We will provide time for each person present to talk if he or she feels comfortable doing so.

   • We will talk about ourselves and our own situations, avoiding conversation about other people.

   • We will listen attentively to each other.

   • We will be very cautious about giving advice.

Additional suggestions for the group leader can be found at the back of the guide.

LONGING TO SEE THE ROMAN CHRISTIANS

Romans 1:1-17

In ancient Rome, as today, the rich people lived up in the hills, the famous seven hills on which the city stands. The original imperial palace, where the emperor Augustus lived at the time when Jesus was born, occupies most of one of them. But then, as now, the poorer people lived in the areas around the river; not least, in the area just across the river from the main city center. And this is where most of the first Roman Christians lived. The chances are that the first time this great letter was read aloud it was in a crowded room in someone's house in the low-lying poorer district, just across the river from the seat of power.

The Roman church consisted of both Jewish believers and Gentile believers. Some of the Jewish Christians were among Paul's closest friends; they would have shared his robust view of how God had fulfilled the Jewish law through the Messiah and also transcended it by including Gentiles on equal terms in his renewed people. But other Jewish Christians would have been deeply suspicious of this: surely God gave the law to Moses? Doesn't that mean that every word of it is valid for all time? Supposing they found themselves living alongside a house-church composed mostly of Gentile Christians who celebrated their freedom from the law, how would they feel? Suspicion, fueled by the social tensions among Rome's cosmopolitan mix of peoples, might easily turn to hostility.

It is into this physical and social context that Paul writes his great letter.

OPEN

In what ways is it risky or daring to be a Christian in your community today?

DIKAI - RIGHTEOUS - JUSTIFY

STUDY

1. *Read Romans 1:1-17.* Like most people writing letters in the classical world, Paul begins by saying who he is, and who the letter is intended for. But, as in some of his other letters, he expands this formula almost beyond the breaking point by adding more and more information on both sides.

   Paul introduces in his greeting several thoughts in verses 1-7 that he will expand on later in the letter. What themes are mentioned?

2. What is the gospel or good news Paul describes in this expanded greeting?

3. In verse 5, Paul uses the term "believing obedience" to depict the goal of the grace and apostleship which Paul and others had received. What does "believing obedience" look like in a Christian's life?

4. Why would news about the faith of the Roman church have spread far and wide?

5. Paul had not himself founded the church in Rome or visited there previously. But as Romans 16 will tell us he had friends and relatives there. Why else does Paul want to visit the Roman Christians so desperately?

6. Caesar's messengers didn't go around the world saying, "Caesar is lord, so if you feel you need to have a Roman Empire kind of experience, you might want to submit to him." Jesus' messengers (or apostles—literally meaning "sent ones") didn't say something indecisive like that about Jesus either.

    In this context, how has Paul already, in this first chapter, proclaimed a rather risky message that might have tempted him or others to be "ashamed of the good news"?

7. How are we tempted to be ashamed of the good news in our own society?

8. The Greeks, who had ruled the world centuries before the Romans, divided the world into two: Greeks and the rest. They called the rest "barbarians," probably because their languages sounded like meaningless mumblings. For a true Greek, the Romans counted as barbarians. But it is a different division of the world that occupies Paul for

the rest of the letter. Jews divided the world into two as well: Jews and the rest. They referred to the rest sometimes as "the nations," sometimes as "Gentiles" and sometimes as "the Greeks," because as far as they were concerned, the rest of the world was Greek-speaking.

How does the good news address the divisions in Rome which Paul highlights in verses 14-17?

9. Does your church reflect the racial barriers common in your community or does it transcend them? Explain how and why.

10. Verse 17 introduces the key word *righteousness* or *justice,* which have the same root. The biblical idea of God's justice is that he will put right all the wrongs of the world. He promised to do this in a covenant he made long ago to Abraham and his family, a promise ultimately realized in Abraham's great descendant, Jesus.

How does the good news about Jesus show God's justice?

11. God has been faithful in keeping his covenant. Now we are called to have faith ourselves in response, as Paul highlights in verse 17. In so doing we enjoy a salvation (v. 16) that provides a rescue from the bonds of death. This means not that we'll all end up in a disembodied heaven, but that God will rescue the entire creation from corruption and decay—and that he will give all his people new bodies, like Jesus' risen body, to live gloriously within his new world.

In addition to providing a future hope, how does salvation also provide a rescue for us from a present reality?

PRAY

Take a few moments to reflect on your own answer to question 3. Then, spend some time praying for one another, that each person would have the strength and courage to live in faith.

NOTE ON ROMANS 1:17

Here Paul introduces a word and theme that will be critical throughout the letter. The Greek word and its variants are often translated as "righteous," "righteousness," "just" or "justice." The problem is that Paul (though writing in Greek) has Hebrew words and meanings in mind, which English translations often overlook. Since these words are frequently misunderstood, and yet are so crucial to Romans, I shall return to this issue at several points in this guide. To begin, I will lay out the basics here. (For more detailed comment see my *Justification: God's Plan and Paul's Vision*, especially chapter 7, published by SPCK and InterVarsity Press.)

Jewish readers of Paul's day would understand the phrase "the righteousness of God" to refer to God's own faithfulness to his promises to Israel, to his covenant (especially as seen in the suffering servant of Isaiah 40—55). He keeps his word and thereby shows his trustworthiness, justice and righteousness.

The word translated "righteousness" comes from the Jewish courts in which there are three parties—the judge, the plaintiff and the defendant. There is no prosecuting attorney, no defense attorney, no jury. Each party makes his case to the judge who is called on to be impartial, to punish wrongdoing and support the defenseless (as called for by the covenant). A judge who acts in this way shows his righteousness, his faithfulness in upholding the covenant.

When the judge finds in favor of either the plaintiff or the defendant, that party is declared "righteous"—not morally good and deserving of a favorable outcome, but one who is given the status by the court of "being in the right" as a result of the judge's decision. The problem is that in Greek and English *righteous* carries moral tones that are not there in the Jewish court system.

What does this mean for what Paul is saying in Romans? The judge does not impart or impute or transfer his righteousness, his just character to either the defendant or the plaintiff. Likewise God, the judge, hears Israel plead her case for vindication against her enemies. She longs to be justified, acquitted, and calls on God to be faithful to his covenant promises to her and do so. When God does act in this way, his people will have gained the court-decreed status of righteousness, but not God's own righteousness, which is instead his covenant faithfulness that Israel by definition cannot share.

As Paul will explain more fully in Romans 3, it is because of God's gracious verdict in Christ that we, Jews and Gentiles, have this new righteous standing. That is the good news Paul says in Romans 1:17 that he is so anxious to announce, for it reveals God's covenant faithfulness to the world.

DARKENED MIND,
DARKENED BEHAVIOR

Romans 1:18—2:16

Imagine a giant beech tree with undiscovered rot inside. If one looks at the tree peripherally, it seems as if nothing is wrong, but if one was to look at the upper branches, there are signs of ill health. Once the tree is cut down and the insides are exposed, the dangerous tree rot is visible. The inside of the trunk is stained with a dark, mottled pattern where the rot had started to spread. Before much longer it would have infected the entire tree. What looks to the casual passerby as a fine, solid old beech could easily have become a serious accident.

Paul's explanation for why the gospel, the unveiling of God's justice and salvation, is urgently required is that the tree is rotten to the core, and might come crashing down at any minute. The tree in question is the human race as it has worked itself into rebellion against its Creator at every level. Humans were always designed to be central to God's plan to rule his creation: that's part of what it means to be made "in God's image" (Genesis 1:26-27). So when humans go wrong, the world as a whole is put out of joint. From Romans 1:18 right through to 2:16, Paul lays out a charge against the human race in general: humankind is rotten at its heart, and the eventual crash to which this will lead is anticipated in the signs of corruption, disintegration and decay.

OPEN

What is one example of the world's corruption, disintegration or decay that was evident to you in the past week?

STUDY

1. *Read Romans 1:18-32.* How, according to Paul in verses 18-23, can all humankind know about God?

2. Just as tree rot spreads throughout the roots and insides of a tree in a progression of destruction, Paul depicts this same process in the hearts of humankind. What is the progression of ungodliness and injustice that is seen in verses 18-23?

3. Where do you see people in the world today claiming to be wise when, in fact, they may be foolish?

4. In verses 24-27, how has human life been distorted from the intentions of God in creation?

5. Taking Genesis 1 as the primary theological statement, Paul sees

humans created in God's image and given charge over the non-human creation. Humans are commanded to be fruitful; they are to celebrate the abundant life-generating capacity of God's good world. And they are charged with bringing God's order to the world, acting as stewards of the garden and all that is in it. Something deep within the structure of the world responds to the coming together of like and unlike, something which cannot be reached by the mere joining together of like and like.

Paul's larger, all-embracing perspective is not that "there are some exceptionally wicked people out there who do revolting things" but "the fact that such clear distortions of the Creator's male-plus-female intention occur in the world indicates that the human race as a whole is guilty of a character-twisting idolatry." It's a sign that the human world in general is out of joint.

The phrase "God gave them up to" is repeated in 1:24, 26 and 28. What does Paul mean by this phrase?

6. In verses 28-32, Paul emphasizes knowledge and an "unfit mind." How does an "unfit mind" lead to the behaviors listed in the rest of this passage?

7. What would it be like to live in a town where all the people were like those described in verses 28-32, especially those depicted in verse 32?

8. *Read Romans 2:1-16.* An elevated pagan moralist, who agrees with Paul about the awful immorality of society and is appalled and shocked about the behavior of others, is the target of Paul's words

in 2:1-11. What is the chink in the armor of that moralist that Paul exposes?

9. What are examples in the news of people who support certain standards of behavior but don't even follow these themselves?

10. Neither Greek nor Roman religion or philosophy had any doctrine of future judgment, but judgment was central to Judaism. Paul places his discussion of the final judgment in the context of this ancient pagan world. How would you summarize Paul's understanding of the final judgment in 2:1-11?

11. Paul proclaims in verse 11 that God shows no partiality in judgment. How does Paul then explain in 2:12-16 how this will be true for both Jews and Gentiles?

12. How does verse 16 bring comfort in the midst of a passage about judgment, where all people, Jews and Gentiles, will be judged according to their lives?

13. What is one thing you can do locally to model God's true justice?

PRAY

In this passage, Paul paints a chilling picture of a world where the hearts and minds of people are darkened and judgment is coming for all people. Even as believers there are areas of our lives that are not yet fully redeemed and, instead, remain ungodly. Spend several minutes in silent confession before the Lord. Focus on asking for forgiveness for these areas of your life that remain ungodly, and ask God to continue the work of redemption.

GOD'S DETERMINED
FAITHFULNESS

Romans 2:17—3:8

The Jews never believed themselves called to be the world's police force (the Romans gave themselves that job), but many of them did believe, because of a repeated theme in their Scriptures, that they were called to be the light of the world. Many, including Paul himself, would have celebrated the fact that God had chosen Israel and given them his law in order to make them a beacon of virtue to the rest of the world. Before his conversion, Paul would have seen this calling of the nation of Israel as the rock on which he could stand firm. He was a Jew; God had called Israel to this position; he was secure.

But Paul had come to see, through his recognition of the crucified Jesus as Messiah, that things were not that easy. A Messiah who led the true Israelites to victory over the pagans would have fit his previous worldview just fine. A Messiah who taught all Israel to obey the Torah perfectly would have been wonderful. But a Messiah who died a shameful death, a criminal's punishment—that meant that the world had turned upside down. This was how God had fulfilled his ancient promises: by having his anointed one killed by the pagans! This bizarre and totally unexpected outcome forced Paul to rethink the role of Israel as a whole, and to factor into this new thinking a strand of prophetic thought which up until then, perhaps, he had left to one side.

OPEN

Describe a time when you were given the responsibility to model or demonstrate something (a behavior, a skill, etc.), but you didn't do well.

STUDY

1. *Read Romans 2:17—3:8.* What is the charge that Paul is making against his fellow Jews—against his former self—in 2:18-24?

2. Paul quotes Isaiah 52:5 in Romans 2:24, drawing on the very center of the prophet's critique of Israel. Israel had not just made a few mistakes but had failed completely in the task God set it. How would Israel's failure affect God's reputation in the world?

The point of Paul's accusations in 2:21-23 is not that he thinks all Jews commit adultery or steal or rob temples. The point is that if even some Jews were doing these things (and, of course, Paul points out that Gentiles do also), this completely undercut Israel's boast that, *as a nation,* it was still the light of the world, able to reveal God's law and truth to the rest of humankind. Israel was failing to fulfill its part in the covenant God made with them, through Abraham, to bring blessing to all nations. What is the solution to this problem? Answering that question is where Paul's argument is headed in the rest of the letter.

3. In 2:25-29, Paul is saying that labels for people, just like for items in a store, can mislead. What are the labels that Paul is talking about and the deception that occurs?

4. How can uncircumcised Gentiles "fulfill the law," as Paul claims they do, when circumcision itself is a requirement of the law (2:26-29)?

5. What does Paul mean when he describes a circumcision of the heart?

6. Once Paul had written the end of chapter 2 he was bound to face the question he asks here at the beginning of chapter 3. If God is creating a "new covenant" people who are to be called "Jew" despite not necessarily being Jewish, and to be referred to as the "circumcision" despite many of them not being circumcised, then what indeed is the point of being Jewish or being circumcised? How does Paul begin to answer this question in 3:1-8?

7. This section of chapter 3 uses the very important term *entrusted*. The point about being "entrusted" is that the thing that's been given to you isn't actually *for* you; it's for the person to whom you are supposed to deliver it. Why is it so crucial for Paul to use this term in these verses?

In Romans 3:3 Paul hits another key point in his argument. Since Israel has failed, will God revoke his plan? Not at all, he says. God still intends to fulfill his promises, his covenant to bring blessing to all the nations *through Israel*. How will that happen? Again, Paul wants us to keep reading.

8. What does Paul emphasize about God in 3:1-8?

9. One of the oldest jibes in the letter to the Romans is found in this section: "Why not simply do what is wrong, so that God, in putting it right, can be seen to be all the greater?" Although Paul does not deal with this question fully until chapter 9, how does he begin to answer it here?

10. As believers we have been entrusted with the gospel of Jesus Christ. How is your life presently fulfilling the calling of being a messenger of the gospel or living as a beacon of light for others to see?

PRAY

Spend some time in silence reflecting on the message that has been entrusted to you. Pray that the way that you treat others, the way that use your time and money, and the state of your heart is a message of the gospel to the world around you. Pray that the name "Christian" and your life are consistent and not deceptive.

THE UNVEILING OF GOD'S COVENANT JUSTICE

Romans 3:9-31

In Paul's world, almost everyone would have been much more familiar with law court proceedings than most people are today. Communities were small and tight-knit. Cases would be tried in public. Everyone would want to see what was going on. So, when Paul uses a lot of law court language, as he does in this passage, everyone would be able to picture the setting he had in mind.

This section of chapter 3 picks up from the rapid-fire discussion in the previous section, which Paul may realize has left some of his listeners gasping for breath, and in effect repeats the question of verse 1: are Jews in fact better off than Gentiles?

OPEN

Think of a time when you were engaged in a dispute of some kind. What was the outcome of the dispute? How did you feel about the end result of the conflict?

STUDY

1. *Read Romans 3:9-31.* What is Paul's purpose in verses 9-20?

2. Why does he choose to quote so much from the Old Testament?

3. Paul is not shy about leveling accusations at his readers through these Old Testament quotations. How does it feel to be confronted (whether by a friend, coworker or stranger) with a wrong you've committed?

4. In Paul's world, if you were on trial and had nothing more to say in your defense, you put a hand over your mouth as a sign. Sometimes court officials would strike the prisoner on the mouth to indicate that their mouths "should be stopped," in other words, that they were obviously guilty and should not be attempting to defend themselves.

   How is this example (v. 19) an appropriate one for the argument Paul is making about both Jews and Gentiles?

5. The advantage the Jews have is being part of God's original covenant promises to bless the nations, as we saw in 3:1-2. But that fact does not enable them to avoid the judgment that hangs over the whole world, as Paul now points out in 3:9-20. He reveals the dilemma which God faces with a human race in rebellion, and a covenant people who are also part of the problem of wickedness. The court

was in session; all were standing guilty in the dock—both Jews who had the law and Gentiles who didn't. Something had to be done.

Paul is now ready to say how God will, apart from the law but not apart from his original plan, still fulfill his covenant promises *through Israel*. In the note on Romans 1:17 at the end of study one, we saw that the "righteousness" or "justice" referred to in Romans 3:21-24 means showing God's faithfulness to the covenant. How does Paul say God did this in verses 21-24?

6. How can the solution be both "apart from the law" and testified to by the law and prophets (v. 21)?

7. When have you received grace from someone when you've fallen short?

8. As said before, the phrase often translated "righteousness of God" in verses 21 and 22 is not, as some have often argued, a righteous quality that God gives or imparts to humans. It is God's own righteousness, his being true to the covenant. This covenant faithfulness carries with it more of the overtones that Paul is trying to highlight, referring back to God's covenant promises to Abraham to undo the problem caused by the sin of Adam. But Israel failed to both keep the law and bring the message of God to the nations.

What does God's fulfillment of his covenant promises to Israel reveal about himself?

9. Some translate key words in verse 22 as "faith in Jesus," but they mean just as easily "the faithfulness of Jesus," referring to Jesus' faithful obedience in fulfilling God's covenant with Israel. What was previously lacking, the faithfulness of Israel, has now been accomplished through the Messiah of Israel. Verse 24 reinforces this by noting that people are justified ("freely declared to be in the right" and given the status of being God's covenant people) through Jesus.

   God's plan for Israel that began with Abraham wasn't scrapped but was fulfilled *through Israel* in the person of the Messiah *of Israel*. By his death, he redeemed (literally, bought back from slavery) his people. How have you experienced freedom in Jesus?

10. In verse 25 Paul combines three references to worship at the temple: "put Jesus forth" or "presented him" (as a priest would put forth the showbread on the altar), the "place of mercy" or the "mercy seat" (the center of God's presence in the Holy of Holies), and the blood (or death) of the sacrificed animal for atonement of sin.

   How do these three images further reveal the way in which God has now, at last, been faithful to his age-old covenant plan?

11. Paul says that Jesus' faithfulness was his dealing with sin to the point of death. How does the death of Jesus show God's willingness to deal with sin when he had earlier left it unpunished, perhaps making him look unjust (v. 26)?

12. In verse 31 Paul says that the law is not abolished. Rather, he says

that the law cannot be fulfilled by works. Instead it is fulfilled by faith. How does reliance on the law of faith instead of the law of works put Jews and Gentiles on the same footing before God?

13. This passage explains the very foundation of the Christian faith. How could you take these verses and restate them in a way that would communicate the message of Christ to people around you who do not know him?

PRAY

Spend several minutes thanking God for his act of mercy in fulfilling the law through Christ and providing a way for all those who have faith in Jesus to be members of the new covenant family. Then, pray for one friend who does not know Jesus. Pray that God would give you opportunities to communicate the message of the gospel in relevant ways.

5

THE FATHER OF
ALL BELIEVERS

Romans 4:1-25

Ohne of the most solemn moments of a wedding ceremony comes when the bride and groom give or exchange rings. The ring declares to the wearer, to the spouse and to the whole wide world that a new relationship has come into being. A new covenant has been made. The ring is a sign and seal of the covenant. It speaks of an endless love, going on and on and on.

When God entered into covenant with Abraham (Genesis 15), he gave him an equivalent. It was the badge of circumcision. Two chapters after the covenant was established, in Genesis 17, God commands Abraham to circumcise himself. It is this story to which Paul refers and threads through all of chapter 4. Here we find not simply an example or illustration of justification by faith but God's very promise to Abraham, which was the foundation of the one plan God had for blessing the whole world through Israel. And what was true when the promise was first given to Abraham continues to be true today.

OPEN

Think about different organizations, groups or institutions that require memberships. What are the signs of membership?

STUDY

1. *Read Romans 4:1-25.* How does Paul's discussion about Abraham, the father of the nation of Israel, follow naturally on the heels of chapter 3?

2. What similar point about how God deals with sin is made by both Romans 4:1-5 and by the quote from Psalm 32 in Romans 4:7-8?

3. In Romans 4:3 and again in 4:9 Paul quotes Genesis 15:6. In 4:9-12 what does Paul point out about when Abraham was circumcised?

4. What Paul means by this "being in the right," this "being declared in the right," this "righteousness" (to use the old, technical term) is essentially the same thing as "membership in the covenant." (See the note on Romans 1:17 at the end of study one.) How then does this notion of "righteousness" fit, in particular, with what Paul says in Romans 3:21-22 about fulfilling the law?

5. This passage was very controversial in Paul's day because in it Paul is redefining the family of Abraham. How has the family of Abraham been redefined both in regard to Gentiles and in regard to Jews in verses 9-12?

6. The church today, and in every generation, must make sure the door is wide enough open to let in people of every ethnic group, every type of family, every geographical region, every sort of moral (or immoral) background. But it must also make sure that the defining characteristic of the membership of this multiethnic family remains firmly stated and adhered to: the faith that Jesus is Lord and that God raised him from the dead.

    How can the church keep this balance and do so in the right spirit?

7. According to Paul in verses 13-15, what is the purpose of the law?

8. How does the knowledge that Abraham is the "father of many nations" (Genesis 17:5) and that you are a child of Abraham affect the way you view your faith?

    Paul is not telling us about something that Abraham (who happens to be our father) had "found," but about *in what sense we have found Abraham to be our father*. The focus for Paul is not "the promise that his sins would be forgiven and that he would go to heaven when he died." It was, rather, *that he would have a family* as numerous as the stars in the heavens (Genesis 15:5).

The point Paul is making is that God, in calling Abraham and promising him innumerable descendants, was thereby acting in sheer grace, irrespective of the fact that Abraham had no merit to commend him. Forgiveness—the nonreckoning of sin—is thus right at the heart of the larger picture which Paul is sketching, but we must not for that reason ignore that larger picture. *The point of God's covenant with Abraham, to give him a single great family, always was that this was how sins would be forgiven, and the initial establishment of that covenant embodied the same principle.* That, if fact, is what God ultimately accomplished in Jesus and thus fulfilled his promise to Abraham.

9. In what specific ways is 4:18-25 a deliberate reversal of Romans 1:18-27?

10. The last verse of the chapter anticipates something Paul is going to do throughout chapters 5 through 8. He rounds off every stage of the argument in this long section with a reference to Jesus. This brings us back home to the source and power of Paul's thought. How do verses 24-25 sum up the previous four chapters of the letter to the Romans?

11. How can we as believers celebrate the God who promises impossible things and brings them to pass?

12. In specific ways, how can we live as one family with all those who share the faith and hope depicted in this chapter?

PRAY

Sit in silence for a few moments and reflect on the impossible things that God has promised to his people. Give God thanks for his power to bring these about. Then, pray for unity in the body of Christ, highlighting particular ways in which the church is not living in unity across ethnic and cultural barriers.

6

THE TRIUMPHANT REIGN OF GRACE

Romans 5:1-21

A published obituary told the story of a comedian who had fallen out with his father when he was still a young man, and the quarrel had never been made up. Then the tragic pattern had repeated itself. One of his own sons had fallen out with him, and had been cut off. Imagine knowing that there is someone there, only a telephone call away, who is one of your closest blood relations . . . and yet he won't speak to you, and you don't want to speak to him. And imagine that going on for years and years. There is something deeply disturbing about the whole picture—and yet not only the man in the obituary but a great many people live exactly like that.

There is even a greater tragedy. A vast number of human beings live exactly like that in relation to God. But here at the center of Romans, Paul talks about a reconciliation to end all reconciliations. Having laid the foundation in chapters 1-4, Paul begins to build the structure: a picture of Christian life in which all the ancient promises of God are coming true. And at the center of these promises is the establishment of a loving, welcoming personal relationship between individual humans and the Creator God himself.

OPEN

What examples can you think of in which a broken relationship was not repaired for a long time?

STUDY

1. *Read Romans 5:1-21.* A key phrase in chapter 5 of Romans is "peace with God." What does peace with God look like as described in verses 1-2?

2. What would the celebrating or rejoicing of verses 2-3 look like in each of the contexts talked about in these verses?

3. How does the progression that is outlined in verses 3-5 build from one point to the next?

4. How are verses 3-5 both difficult and hopeful for us as we live out the Christian faith in the world today?

5. Paul constantly keeps in mind how justification or being "declared to be in the right" works out in practice. Describe the past, present and future aspects of the work of God in verses 6-11.

6. Paul's argument in verses 6-11 takes the form—familiar in various systems of logic, not least Jewish ones—of a "how much more." If someone has struggled up a sheer rock face, against all odds, to get to the top of the mountain, they are not likely to give up when, at the top of the vertical wall, they are faced with an easy stroll on a grassy path. How does this analogy explain verses 9-11?

7. The logic of "how much more" continues in Paul's discussion of Adam and Jesus in verses 12-17. How is the work of the one man, Jesus, far beyond the effect of the sin of the one man, Adam?

8. Paul uses "reign" three times in verses 12-17. Discuss the distinctions between the types of "reign." Who is reigning and what does that look like?

9. How do verses 18-21 summarize the entire letter of Romans so far?

10. The idea of a beautiful and good world, spoiled at one point in time by human rebellion, remains basic to all early Christian, as to all Jewish, thought. The picture of humankind in a state of sin is indeed a sorry one. In what ways do verses 18-21 contradict the view of humanity that society today holds?

11. Think about an area of your life, your community or the world that demonstrates the brokenness of sin. What would that area look like if there was a "reign of grace" instead of a reign of death?

PRAY

Spend some time praying for the area that was identified in question eleven. Paul tells us that those who have received membership in the covenant will reign in life. Pray that you will reign in life in this area of the community or the world.

7

DEAD TO SIN, ALIVE TO GOD

Romans 6:1-23

The story of the prodigal son is a familiar one (Luke 15:11-32). The younger son twists his father's arm for his share of the property, goes off and spends it all, and comes home, he thinks, in utter disgrace. Then, to his astonishment, he finds his father running down the road to meet him, and throwing a huge party in his honor. He is welcomed back as a son, even though he doesn't deserve it (and even though his older brother grumbles).

Now come forward a year or two, and imagine a thought stealing unbidden into the young man's mind. Life has settled down to a reasonably humdrum existence again. His older brother tolerates having him around, more or less; his father is getting older. He remembers with a happy sigh the day he came up the road and his father came running to greet him . . . and he thinks, supposing I did it again? Why not help myself to enough things to survive, run away for a few weeks, and then play the penitent and come back again? Maybe I'll get another party!

Absurd? Unthinkable? Don't you believe it. It's exactly what a great many people think. "God will forgive me; that's his job." Paul probably met exactly this line of argument again and again. Chapter 6 is written, at one level at least, to answer this point.

OPEN

Think of someone you know who has inspiring talents and abilities but is not a follower of Christ. What would they be like and what impact could they have for Christ if they became a Christian?

STUDY

1. *Read Romans 6:1-23.* The book of Exodus tells the story of how the children of Israel were enslaved in Egypt. God heard them crying in misery in Egypt, so he sent Moses to bring them out. God led them through the Red Sea to Mount Sinai where they left behind their life of slavery. The Israelites wandered in the wilderness, but God continued to lead them by his presence until they entered the Promised Land.

   Here in Romans, Paul tells a version of this story. Where do you see echoes of the Exodus story in 6:1-5?

2. How does Paul proceed to answer the question he raises in 6:1?

3. What is Paul's understanding of baptism in 6:1-5?

4. According to Paul's argument in these first five verses, a believer has experienced a change of status. What is required of those with this new status?

5. How do verses 6-14 describe the true identity of a believer in Christ?

6. The word in verse 11 that is translated as "calculate" or "count" is a word that is used in bookkeeping, in calculating accounts, in working out profit and loss figures. What might be the purpose of Paul using this term in verse 11?

7. How is presenting or offering your limbs and organs to God (v. 13) different from presenting them to sin?

8. What is involved in becoming a Christian, and then living the life of God's renewed humanity, is a change of master. How can we present ourselves to God when we still seem to be under sway of the wrong master?

9. Paul continues with the idea of slavery in verses 15-19, but exhorts his readers that they are "enslaved to God's covenant purposes" and they are to present their "limbs and organs as slaves to covenant justice." How do these terms explain a fuller understanding of the life of the faith?

10. What does it mean that believers are to "become obedient from the heart to the pattern of teaching to which you were committed" (v. 17)?

11. Paul moves from the analogy of slavery to an analogy of roads. Describe the two "destinations" that Paul speaks of in verses 20-23.

12. Slavery to sin or to God and his covenant purposes, embracing our true identity as freed from sin, and presenting ourselves fully to covenant justice are all main ideas in chapter 6. Imagine if Paul were to look up for a moment from writing this letter and glance round the church, maybe your church, at the start of the twenty-first century. What might he say regarding these themes?

PRAY

Pray specifically for yourself and others in the areas raised by questions 7 and 8. Pray for freedom from the control of the wrong master and for the strength to live in the true identity of Christ.

8

LIFE UNDER THE LAW

Romans 7:1-25

The house was quiet when the workmen arrived, and when someone came to the door, they assumed it was the owner himself. The workmen had come to install a new alarm system on the doors and windows. The owner had been anxious about burglaries, following a spate of break-ins in the neighborhood, and had called the company to come and set up a better system than his present one.

But the owner was ill on the day the work was to be done, and he had called a neighbor to answer the door while he was out of action. The neighbor went round the house with the workmen and learned exactly how the alarm system worked. Which gave him an idea . . . and of course put him in an ideal position to burgle the house himself. There was nothing wrong with the alarm system. Indeed, it was excellent. But it put the idea in the neighbor's mind and enabled him to bring it off.

The story makes a good illustration of the points Paul will make in chapter 7 of Romans. The present chapter, though very difficult, is essential if we are to grasp the depth of the human problem and hence the wonder of God's solution to it.

OPEN

Discuss a time in your life when you desperately wanted to act in a manner that you felt was right but you just could not seem to act in this way.

STUDY

1. *Read Romans 7:1-25.* What contrasts does Paul use throughout this chapter?

2. In verses 1-6, Paul tries to illustrate some main points about the law, by which he means the law of Moses given to the Israelites on Mount Sinai. How is the law a part of the problem for Israel rather than the solution (see vv. 1-11)?

3. Describe the differences between the two types of fruit referenced in verses 4 and 5.

4. Give examples of how you've seen each kind of fruit recently.

5. People in the ancient world often wrote in the first-person singular ("I") when they wanted to say something more general. There are several good reasons for supposing that this is what Paul is doing in the rest of the chapter, rather than transcribing his own struggles

with the law. He is not talking about the human race but about Israel, in particular.

How can the law as depicted in verses 7-12 be holy, good and upright while also producing death at the same time?

6. In verses 7-12, Paul describes the time when the law arrived in Israel in such a way as to reflect also the time when Adam was given the commandment in the Garden (Genesis 2:15-17; 3:1-7). What are the similarities between the story in Genesis and Paul's argument here?

7. Because much of the discussion in chapter 7 is about Israel, it may seem remote to many modern Christians. Many of us do not stop to ponder the situation of Israel under the law—though perhaps we should. How is this section relevant to us as believers today?

8. Verses 13-20 are often misunderstood, and many Christians struggle to discern the period of Paul's life that is being described in this passage. But these verses were not intended as an exact description of Paul's, or anyone else's, actual experience, though it finds echoes in many places both in human life and in ancient and modern literature. In these verses, Paul moves into the present tense, to describe the actual situation (as opposed to the felt experience) of Israel living under the law.

Granting this perspective, what happens when Israel, having been given the law, does its best to live under it?

9. Why would God (who is often implicated in Paul's "in order that" clauses) want sin to grow to its full height (v. 13)?

10. What dilemma does Paul highlight in the closing verses of the chapter (vv. 21-24)?

11. How is Jesus the solution to the problem for Israel?

12. What do God's desire, plan and fulfillment through Jesus to rescue us from this dilemma reveal to you about God's character and purposes?

PRAY

Take some time to simply praise God for his act of mercy in his rescue of you and others you know. Praise him for his attributes, his power and his compassion.

9

CHILDREN OF GOD, LED BY THE SPIRIT

Romans 8:1-17

Imagine rummaging around in an old attic and coming upon what looks like a standard lamp. It has a very strange type of bulb but an elegant stem; and the shade, though a bit dusty, is quite attractive. You bring it down into the house and consider it. If you didn't know very much about the history of lamps, you might even try attaching it to the electrical outlets. If you did, you would probably get a shock, literally and metaphorically. This lamp isn't designed to run on electricity. It is the old type; it was made for gas.

An unlikely tale, perhaps, but it highlights the point that Paul is making in these verses. It is no good running the current, the "life," through the wrong sort of appliance; you may just get an explosion. It must be run through an appliance of the right sort, one designed to work in the same mode. It must be applied to someone whose very being and identity has been changed.

OPEN

Who do you know who has been adopted or has adopted? How has this process affected the people involved?

STUDY

1. *Read Romans 8:1-17.* When Paul begins this section of Romans with "therefore," he indicates there is a connection between what he has just said and what he goes on to say. How does Romans 8:1-4 connect with the main themes found in Romans 7?

2. Paul declares exuberantly that "there is no condemnation for those in the Messiah, Jesus!" No condemnation! This assurance can of course only carry its full force for someone who has pondered carefully the seriousness of sin and the reality of God's judgment. What words of Paul's in Romans so far have given you a deeper picture of the seriousness of sin and the reality of God's judgment?

3. According to Paul, sin has received its death-wound. Before the Spirit can be unleashed to blow like a spring gale through the dead wood of the world, the power of evil needs to be broken. The way that needs to happen is for sin to be condemned—not just the passing of sentence but its execution.

   How, according to 8:1-4, has this "execution" happened?

4. In the Old Testament, a sin offering (mentioned in v. 3 here) was a sacrifice used when someone committed a sin unwittingly (not knowing it was wrong) or unwillingly (knowing it was wrong but not intending to do it)—the very kinds of sin Paul considers in Romans 7. How is this image of a sin offering helpful to Paul's line of thought in verses 1-4?

5. In verses 5-11 Paul moves into an extended contrast between what is flesh and what is the Spirit. He isn't talking about "material" versus "nonmaterial," since for Paul as a Jew the physical created order was good. From what Paul says here then, define what he means by these terms.

6. How does Paul say you can tell the difference between those who are concerned with "flesh" and those concerned with "the Spirit"?

7. Give some examples of what it might look like to live life concerned with the things of the Spirit.

8. Paul has not developed a regular formula for speaking about God as one in three, but he already possessed all the elements that would later be known as "trinitarian theology." How are God the Father, God the Son and God the Holy Spirit seen in verses 5-11?

9. One of the most terrible things about debt is that it dominates your mind. Whatever else you might be going to think of, or plan or hope for, the fact that you're in debt determines the way you see the world. So, why does Paul so dramatically begin verses 12-17 by saying we have an obligation or are in debt?

10. These verses take us into territory where we have been before in

Romans. Paul begins to echo the story of the exodus in which the nation of Israel traveled out of slavery in Egypt, was led by God through the wilderness, became tempted to return to Egypt when things got hard but ultimately moved toward the Promised Land. How is the book of Exodus glimpsed in verses 12-17?

11. What are the privileges of being "led by the Spirit" in verses 14-17?

12. Paul explains that the Christian discovers a new identity, picking up Israel's vocation in the Old Testament: adoption. How is adoption a wonderful image for the work of God in the lives of believers?

13. Paul begins this last section by saying that we are in debt, not to the "flesh" but to God. We have to live in a particular way, a way which anticipates the "glory," the rule over creation, which we will eventually share with the Messiah. How can you live this week in the specific knowledge of being in debt to God?

PRAY

Sit in silence, giving thanks and praise for being in debt not to sin and death but to God. Then offer short prayers of thanksgiving, giving glory to God for adopting us as his children.

NOTHING SHALL
SEPARATE US

Romans 8:18-39

The woods were thick, with paths leading this way and that. I knew some of them quite well, and had my favorites among them. But there was another path which I had never taken. It looked a bit overgrown and I couldn't see where it would go. Until one day I came past the place, and someone had cleared the bushes enough to reveal a post with four letters, and an arrow pointing along the path. Down the post starting with a *V* were *I, E* and *W*. A *view*? What sort of a view? Intrigued, I took the path for the first time.

To begin with, it was as I'd expected: overgrown with brambles, thorns in the way and muddy underfoot. But then it turned sharply through the trees and began to climb quite steeply. Suddenly, instead of thick trees all around me, I saw clear sky emerging. Then I was out of the trees and onto a slab of rock. It was indeed a view. I was looking down not only on the whole large wood but also on the little town beyond it. I could see other hills in the distance and smoke rising from the villages in between. Half the country seemed to lie there before me. And I might never have known.

Romans 8:18-39 is like that view. From this point we can see the whole plan of salvation for all of God's creation. Once you've glimpsed this view, you will never forget.

OPEN

What is it about the world that makes you "groan" in frustration, anger or desperation for something to change?

STUDY

1. *Read Romans 8:18-39.* In these verses, creation plays a key part in Paul's words. Describe all the things that creation is experiencing and "doing" in verses 18-25.

2. What is "the glory that is going to be unveiled for us" depicted in verse 18?

3. Paul repeats several key terms in this passage, one of which is *groaning.* Who is groaning in these verses and why?

4. We often fail to appreciate how central this dramatic climax is in a chapter which is the climax of Paul's letter so far. When we look at the world of creation as it is in the present, we see a world in the same condition as the children of Israel were in when they were enslaved in Egypt. There were summer and winter, growth and decay, birth and death. Beautiful, yes, but futile slavery nonetheless.

The whole created order shows the effects of the sin found in Genesis 3, and God always intended to put the world back right. That is the vision Paul opens to us here. The whole creation is waiting—on tiptoe with expectation, in fact—for the freedom it will enjoy when God gives to his children the glory of wise rule and stewardship of creation which was always intended for those who bear God's glorious image. Just as our fallen, frail bodies will ultimately be resurrected in a physical form that cannot die, so creation itself looks forward to its own transformation as the new earth with the new heaven.

What are the implications for us now as individuals and as a society, knowing that creation itself looks forward to this transformation?

5. How are the hope and patient waiting in verses 18-25 connected to the mention of suffering in verse 18 and in the previous chapter?

6. Verse 27 calls God a "Searcher of Hearts." In the context of 8:26-30, what does this powerful but mysterious name imply?

What is he searching for?

7. In verses 18-27 we see that the world is in pain, groaning in the birth pangs of new creation. We see too that the church shares this pain, groaning in our longing for our own redeemed bodies, suffering in the tension between the "already" of possessing the first fruits of the

Spirit and the "not yet" of our present moral existence. The church is not to be separated from the pain of the world; now we discover that God himself does not stand apart from the pain both of the world and the church, but comes to dwell in the middle of it in the person and power of the Spirit.

How does the knowledge that this kind of intercession is happening in us between God and the Spirit affect your perspective on life and the world?

8. What are the various dimensions of the purpose to which we are called in verses 28-30?

9. Which of these dimensions strikes you most and why?

10. In verses 31-39 the same question is asked in four slightly different ways and then answered each time, creating a sustained excitement, like a symphony entering its final moments. The paragraph is, in fact, a summary of the major themes of Romans 5—8.

   Summarize the question that is asked and the answers that are offered.

11. How are these last verses of Romans 8 a great assurance for us in the tension of life and the suffering of the world?

12. Think about your answer to the opening question. In what ways
    does this passage speak to you in regard to your answer?

PRAY

Spend a few moments sitting and waiting on the Lord in prayer. Then
ask the Spirit to intercede on your behalf for the areas of personal and/
or shared suffering that come to mind. Allow the Spirit to groan in deep
prayer, perhaps, in ways that are new or unfamiliar.

11

GOD'S PURPOSE
AND JUSTICE

Romans 9:1-29

W hen you walk or drive through unfamiliar territory, you have to rely on the map. It is the bottom line. If you find yourself somewhere you didn't expect, you scratch your head, get out the map again and figure out where you went wrong. You mistook *that* turning for *this* one . . . so you took the road that went over *there* instead of over *here* . . . so no wonder you've landed up on the wrong side of the river. You'll have to go back and start again from the place where you made the mistake. It is, of course, possible in theory that the map might be wrong. Mapmakers are fallible human beings like the rest of us. But if that's so, then you really are lost. There's nothing you can trust.

What we see in Romans 9 is Paul going back to the beginning of the map and starting again. Jewish thinkers in his day often retold the story of Israel, beginning with Abraham or even with Adam, in order to explain the whole sequence of God's actions in their history up to the present day and even beyond. Paul is doing something similar. Here he tells, from one surprising angle, the story of Abraham, Isaac and Jacob—and of Ishmael and Esau as well—in order to explain what the map (God's word of promise) has in mind all along. He had misread it, he now believes, and is eager to help others who had misread it in the same way.

OPEN

Think of something you have made with your own hands (a work of art, a meal, a piece of furniture, etc.). What was your purpose in making it? How did you feel about it once it was done?

STUDY

1. *Read Romans 9:1-29.* What seems to be the tone of this chapter? What is Paul feeling as he writes this section of his letter?

2. What is the cause of Paul's emotions in verses 1-5?

3. What can be learned from Paul's attitudes in verses 1-5 about how we're to respond to the Jewish people today?

4. People have often imagined that Romans 9—11 are a kind of digression, an appendix, tackling a different subject to the rest of the letter. But that only shows how badly Romans as a whole has been misread. The whole letter is about the way God is fulfilling his ancient promises to Abraham in and through Jesus, and what this will mean in practice, both to Jews and to those of every race and nation.

In 9:6 Paul says that it can't be that God's word has failed. How might bringing Gentiles into God's family through Jesus have made the Jews wonder if God's promises to them had failed?

5. Paul assumes his readers of this letter know the story of the book of Genesis, that God promised to Abraham to bless all the nations through his descendants. He assumed they knew that Abraham had two sons (Isaac by his wife Sarah and Ishmael by Sarah's maid Hagar) and that Isaac had twin sons (Esau and Jacob by his wife Rebekah). He assumes they knew that God chose Isaac rather than Ishmael and that he chose Jacob rather than Esau.

   Based on this history, what conclusion does Paul draw in verses 6-13 about how people do and don't become children of God?

6. Paul is making the case that all the physical descendants of Abraham never automatically shared equally in the calling of Abraham. From the beginning that promise was narrowed down to the line of just one of two of Abraham's sons (Isaac). The promise further narrowed to just one of two sons of Isaac (Jacob). This narrowing process is nothing new. It's the way God has always worked, Paul says. Indeed in light of the overall failure of Israel, God has seen fit to continue this process by having the ultimate fulfillment narrowed down to just one descendant of Abraham—Jesus, the Messiah—through whom God's promise to bless all the nations would be accomplished.

   How does this make Paul's case that God hasn't changed his mind (or broken his word) about the Jews but that, from the beginning, he has treated them (and his promise to them) the same way as always?

7. In verses 14-18 Paul continues his review of the whole history of Israel. He began in verses 6-13 with Abraham, Isaac and Jacob. Now he references Moses' encounter with Pharaoh some four hundred years later and Israel's exodus from Egypt. The story in Exodus 33 is where God declares to Moses that he will proceed with his plan for the exodus even though the people have made the golden calf, amounting to a declaration of independence from the true God. This is the setting for verse 15 in particular.

    Why is this story in Exodus significant to Paul's argument in chapter 9?

8. Then in verses 19-29 Paul moves on to the period of the prophets several hundred years after the exodus. He recalls the image of a potter and clay from Isaiah 29:16, 45:9 and Jeremiah 18:1-6, which tell of a stage in Israel's history when God was struggling with rebellious Israel.

    How is the image of a potter and clay helpful in understanding God's attitude toward sinful Israel and the purpose he had for it to be a means of blessing to others?

9. After Jeremiah, Israel went into exile in Babylon, because of its sin, where it was reshaped by God. The alternatives, after all, would seem to be that God would, on the one hand, simply ignore Israel's

rebellion and proceed with an automatic "favored nation clause," which Paul has already firmly ruled out in chapter 2—or, on the other hand, that God would scrap the plan and the promises altogether, which again is ruled out by God's own character.

In the context of the whole passage, why would Paul's idea of "vessels of mercy" in verse 23 mean not so much vessels which receive mercy, but a vessel through which God brings mercy to others?

10. How do verses 25-29 also emphasize Paul's point that God is faithful to his promises to Israel?

11. How do these verses respond to the charge that God is not just?

12. God has to reshape Israel because of their failure to live out the purpose to which they had been called, just as a potter molds a lump of clay for his own ends. The church has also been called to a purpose in the world. What is that purpose and how well is the church living this out?

13. What needs to happen for your Christian community to live out its purpose more strongly?

PRAY

Confess ways in which the church has not responded well to Jewish people. Continue with confession over specific ways the church has not lived out its calling. End by praying for the church worldwide, in the nation and in your particular fellowship, to more fully live out its calling.

NOTE ON ROMANS 9:13

Many people feel uneasy reading these verses, particularly verse 13. It seems that Paul has managed to rescue God from the charge of incompetence, of failing to do what he promised, only to land him instead into a much worse one, of flagrant favoritism and injustice. Paul is as well aware of this question as we are, as 9:14 shows.

But we should reflect, as well, on what Malachi himself meant when he said that God loved Jacob but hated Esau. There was no question that God had done remarkable things for Israel, Jacob's family, while Edom, the family of Esau, had collapsed into insignificance. But the point the prophet Malachi was making (and the point the whole book of Malachi— which criticizes Israel harshly—was making) was that Israel's responsibility, and culpability, is now increased.

The thrust was not, You are special so you can sit back and take it easy. It was always instead, You are special, so why are you taking God for granted, failing to honor him, and ignoring your call to carry forward his purposes? God's choice never results in easy, arrogant, automatic superiority. Much is expected of those to whom much is given.

12

THE FULFILLMENT OF THE COVENANT

Romans 9:30—10:21

An architect can be very helpful in designing a house. But if the plan doesn't match the owner's intentions, there is bound to be trouble.

That's the situation Paul is describing in this passage. Israel has behaved like an architect trying to design God's people and God's plan the way it wants instead of the way God wants. Faced with this, Paul has a double task. Not only must he explain what God's original plan had been, he must also explain how even Israel's failure to believe was foreseen in Israel's scriptures themselves.

Paul makes clear that the apparently strange design the owner had for the house—Gentiles flooding into God's people, many Israelites deliberately staying out—had been drawn into the blueprint all along.

OPEN

Do you long for certain people to find God? What is the substance of your prayers for them?

STUDY

1. *Read Romans 9:30—10:21.* As we look at the word in 9:30—10:4 that is often translated as "righteousness," we need to remember that what Paul has in mind is not "uprightness" but "covenant membership," "covenant faithfulness," "covenant status" and "faithfulness." (See the note on Romans 1:17 at the end of study one.) So 10:3-4 is better translated, "They were ignorant, you see, of God's covenant faithfulness, and they were trying to establish a covenant status of their own; so they didn't submit to God's faithfulness. The Messiah, you see, is the goal of law, so that covenant membership may be available for all who believe."

   How do these ideas connect with Paul's argument in 9:1-13 about Gentiles and Jews being God's children?

2. Read Isaiah 28:16 and Isaiah 8:14, which Paul combines in Romans 9:33. Looking at Romans 9:30—10:4, what is Paul trying to communicate by saying that Christ, the Messiah, is both a stumbling block and a reliable rock?

3. In 10:4 Paul says the Messiah, Christ, "is the goal of the law." Christ is the end, the final purpose of the law, where God's purposes that began with Abraham were headed all along. The purpose of the law is not to accumulate a treasury of moral merit, but it is the assured status of belonging to God's people.

   How does Christ accomplish the purpose of the law?

4. *Read Deuteronomy 30:11-14,* which Paul mentions in Romans 10:6-8. Deuteronomy 28—30 come near the end of Moses' long charge to the Israelites before they enter the Promised Land. There Moses tells Israel what is going to happen to them in the days to come. If Israel keeps God's commandments, God promises blessings; if they don't, he warns of curses to come. What's more, Moses solemnly predicts that Israel *will* disobey and will be driven out of the Promised Land, sent off into exile.

   But then Deuteronomy 30 has a fresh word, a further promise to which God commits himself. He promises to transform their hearts, so that they can at last keep his law the way he always intended.

   In Romans 10:5-13 how is Paul suggesting that what Moses said about Israel's disobedience and exile, as well as the promise of a new word, have been fulfilled in Jesus?

5. In Paul's world, "Lord" was a title for Caesar. Saying Jesus was "Lord" meant, ultimately, that Caesar was not. Today, when we say Jesus is Lord, who or what are we saying is *not* Lord?

6. In what ways were Paul (quoting Isaiah 52:7) and the apostles who went to the Gentiles with the gospel fulfilling the traditions of Israel rather than being disloyal to them (10:13-15)?

7. In 10:16 Paul goes back to the question that has caused him such anguish, "Why are so many of the Jews refusing to believe in the

Messiah?" In a series of Old Testament quotations who does Paul, playing the lawyer, call as witnesses against the Jews, and what is significant about each piece of testimony (10:16-21)?

8. How does Paul also make the case that even Scripture itself foresaw that those who weren't even looking for salvation from Israel's God would stumble into it?

9. What would make the Jews jealous and angry toward the Gentiles according to 10:16-21?

10. God made his basic promises of salvation to Israel; Israel clung on to them, often in the belief that they were for their nation and nobody else. But (as Paul has stressed over and over in this letter) the promises were intended to work *through* Israel for the benefit of the rest of the world.

    The gospel burst upon the Gentiles unawares, like someone announcing the end of a long and bitter war to people who hadn't even heard what was going on. Gentiles, too, belonged in the one creation of the one God, and what God had done for Israel had immediate implications for the whole world.

    In what ways has the gospel burst into your life unexpectedly?

11. At the end of this chapter of Romans we do well to stop and ponder the strange path by which the gospel first made its way into the world, humbling the proud and lifting up the lowly. Is this what happens with the preaching of the gospel today? If not, why not?

PRAY

Spend time praying for the people named in the opening question. Pray that there would be people who are sent to them to announce the gospel. Pray that the gospel would burst upon their lives unawares, and that their response would be to profess Christ's lordship with their mouths and believe in their hearts that they will be saved.

THE REMNANT OF GRACE

Romans 11:1-36

This place isn't big enough for both of us!" We've all heard it, or perhaps even said it. Sometimes it's in an office where two managers both want their plans to go ahead. Sometimes it's in a sports team where two players both want to be the star. Sometimes, tragically, it's in a home where two squabbling teenagers both want to run things their way.

It's even uglier when this kind of rivalry gets played out in a church; and that's what Paul is anxious about here in chapter 11.

OPEN

How do Christian believers who aren't ethnically Jewish respond to the Jewish people today?

STUDY

1. *Read Romans 11:1-36.* Once again Paul raises the question of whether God has abandoned Israel and perhaps broken his promise to them. In verses 1-6 Paul uses the story of Elijah (from 1 Kings 18—19).

How are Paul and Elijah similar?

2. The idea of a "remnant," a few people who remain after a great disaster, comes from the heart of the Old Testament, from Isaiah 10:20-23 where the prophet describes those who will return after the punishment of exile. Who is the remnant Paul has in mind?

3. What is the situation of the Jews to whom Paul is referring in verses 7-12?

4. Verses 7-15 (and all of Romans 9—11) echo the stories of tensions between younger and older brothers from Genesis (Cain and Abel, Ishmael and Isaac, Esau and Jacob, Joseph and his brothers) as well as Jesus' own parable of the prodigal son in Luke 15. In all these cases God establishes and vindicates the younger over the older. How is Israel now in the position of being the older brother in the prodigal son story?

5. How might jealousy, as described in verses 11-15, actually draw Jews to Christ?

6. Paul sees Israel's blindness and stumbling (vv. 8-10) as a means by which the wider world can be brought into God's family (vv. 11-12).

How is it that Paul nonetheless has hope for Israel's future and envisions its resurrection (vv. 11-15)?

7. Beginning in verse 13 and continuing through verse 32 Paul is speaking directly to the Gentile Christians in the Roman church. What seems to be the danger in the Gentile believers that Paul is addressing?

What is his warning to them?

8. He uses two illustrations in verses 16-24 to highlight the point he wants to make to the Gentile believers. What is Paul saying here?

9. One thing that many people may not know about olive trees in ancient Israel is that, from time to time, gardeners performed grafting operations on them. Some olives grew wild, and would often be quite strong in themselves though not producing good fruit. The gardener might decide to take that energy and harness it by grafting shoots from a proper, cultivated olive into the trunk of a wild olive, thus combining the energy of the wild tree and the fruitfulness of the cultivated one.

Why does Paul reverse the illustration?

10. How is God's mercy showered on all in verses 25-32?

11. Verses 33-36 end chapter 11 by using the rich traditions of Hebrew praise from Isaiah and Job. How does Paul want us to feel and respond at the end of this amazing discussion of God's grace and his covenant faithfulness?

12. Once Israel arrogantly assumed it was the sole repository of God's mercy and blessing. Paul warns the Gentiles against a similar arrogance in Romans 11:20. How does the danger of arrogance, which was a temptation for Jews and Gentile Christians alike, seep into our churches today?

How are you tempted by it in your own life?

PRAY

Focus the prayer time on praising God for his mercy on all and his grace through Jesus Christ. Praise will keep us humble and protect us from the arrogance which destroys Christian community.

NOTE ON ROMANS 11:26

How is "all Israel" going to be saved? Many people find this verse puzzling. Surely, they say, "all Israel" must mean "all Jews"—either all Jews who have ever lived, or all believing Jews, or all Jews alive at the time of final salvation. But Paul himself has indicated otherwise.

At the very start of the discussion, in the passage beginning at 9:6, he has declared that "not all who are of Israel are in fact of Israel." In a similar passage in Galatians (6:16), he has spoken of the "Israel of God," meaning the whole family of the Messiah—Jew and Gentile alike (see also Galatians 3:26-29). Some translations of Romans, assuming that verse 26 refers to all *Jews* being saved, make it sound as though Paul here refers to a fresh event which comes *after* the event at the end of verse 25, but that's not what Paul says. In verse 25 he is saying that "a hardening has come upon Israel, allowing time for the nations to come in; *and that is how* God is saving 'all Israel.'"

The phrase "all Israel shall be saved" was already something of a regular slogan in some Jewish thinking; Paul here takes it and widens its scope. All Israel? That means all the family of Abraham—and that includes believing Gentiles as well as believing Jews (Romans 4:16).

THE LIVING SACRIFICE

Romans 12:1-21

The seven friends had discovered that they were all interested in gardens, to the point of being ready to give up their various jobs and work together at a new business. There wasn't a proper garden center for twenty miles; there was clearly a hole in the market. But who was going to do what?

Geoffrey and Ruth were the natural leaders with business and financial experience, so the rest agreed that they should coordinate the whole project. Thomas was itching to start growing things, especially vegetables, and he was delighted when the group agreed that he should look after that section. Rebecca was a keen gardener and would look after the flowers and the shrubs. Gerry was one of nature's handymen; they were going to need him all right. And Richard? What could he do? He wasn't good with his hands, and was not very keen on business. But he was everyone's best friend, the one who made them all cheerful. They all realized that he could be the key person in the main office, greet people as they came in, organize all the paperwork and write reports. The business was launched.

If only it could be like that in the church. But, according to Paul in Romans 12, it should be!

OPEN

Describe the gifts that you believe God has graciously given you that are
or can be an asset to your community of faith. Don't be shy about shar-
ing the wonderful ways God has gifted you.

STUDY

1. *Read Romans 12:1-21.* What does it mean to be "living sacrifices" (v. 1)?

    During the 'living' of our daily lives to the Lord.

2. Why does Paul emphasize the mind in verse 2?

    Because the mind controls what we do (the body) + it needs to be renewed or 'restored' -

3. How do Paul's words in verses 3-5 help Christians be more unified
    in one body?

    We all have gifts + should not only contribute our gifts but recog the gifts of others + how they all are necessary & fit together

4. In verses 6-13, how does Paul suggest that the gifts he mentions are
    not just ways in which we are carried away by supernatural power
    but that they also involve plain hard work?

    We should contribute so the church functions as it was meant to.

5. How, according to Paul, might our attitude make a big difference as
    we express our gifts? *We need to be content with what our gifts are + eager to use them in work for God.*

6. What do you find particularly challenging in verses 6-13?

   Meeting tribulation with triumphant fortitude

7. How does this chapter so far (vv. 1-13) relate to what Paul has just been talking about in the previous chapters of Romans?

   Works

8. In verses 14-21 Paul does not intend to say that believers should "go soft on evil." Saying you shouldn't take revenge isn't a way of saying evil isn't real, or that it didn't hurt after all, or that it doesn't matter. Evil *is* real; it often *does* hurt, sometimes very badly indeed and with lasting effects, and it *does* matter.

   What does Paul say we are to do about evil?

   As Christ did - forgive + pray for them.

9. What happens when people do start engaging in private vengeance?

   The Lord holds the ultimate vengeance - We set a very bad example when we undertake vengeance

10. How can a society make sure this doesn't happen?

11. How is Christ himself an example of living out what Paul calls for in verses 14-21?

    Crying out for our forgiveness as He was being crucified.

12. The early part of Romans 12 (vv. 1-13) deals with what we might call the inner life of the church. This last section (vv. 14-21) is about how Christians behave within the wider public world. How would the wider world respond to seeing the church live out what's described in 14-21?

It would be more compelling then anything else we could do

13. In what specific ways can you be a "living sacrifice" to those around you right now?

PRAY

Bring to God topics you raised in the answers to questions 6 and 13. Listen for the Spirit to lead you as you pray.

LOVE, THE LAW
AND THE COMING DAY

Romans 13:1-14

Many people today take it for granted that political leaders are not to be trusted. Many Christians take it for granted that governments are corrupt and dehumanizing, and that it's part of our brief as followers of the Lord Jesus, the world's true sovereign, that we should offer serious criticism and opposition, even, if necessary, at a cost to our own prospects.

When Paul was writing during the first century, the Roman Empire was ruled by the notorious Nero. The system he ran was full of injustice and imperial arrogance, and had been for a long time. Some people find it so incredible that Paul in Romans 13 would endorse such submission to governments that they wonder if maybe the paragraph has been stuck in to the letter by someone else. Other people think that this may have been a topic Paul hadn't given much thought to at this stage, but that by the time he wrote later letters from prison he had changed his mind about whether Roman authority was such a good thing.

These explanations are not convincing. Indeed, they miss the point of what's going on. Of course, this paragraph has been used—and abused— by many people in power as a way of telling their subjects to keep silent and offer no resistance even in the face of flagrant abuse. Like many pas-

sages in the Bible, a few verses taken out of context can become dangerous and misleading. When we put these verses back into their context,
right here in the letter, we start to see what Paul is getting at.

OPEN

What happens in a society when there are no properly accredited and
generally recognized rulers? What examples can you give?

STUDY

1. *Read Romans 13:1-14.* According to Paul in verses 1-5, what is to be
   the role of government?

2. Paul describes the "ruling power" as "God's servant" twice in these
   verses. How can government be a servant of God?

3. *Read Acts 16:35-40 and 23:1-3.* How can what Paul says in Romans
   13:1-7 regarding government be reconciled with Paul having no hes-
   itation in telling authorities they are acting illegally or unjustly?

4. At this point in history, the Christians in Rome were considered
   very problematic by the Roman authorities. Why would Paul's ex-
   hortations to the believers in verses 1-7 be important in this cultural
   context?

5. In this passage Paul stands within a particular Jewish tradition from the Old Testament. The Old Testament had denounced pagan nations and their rulers—but some of the very prophets whose denunciations were fiercest also told Israel that God was working *through* the pagan nations and their rulers for Israel's long-term good (Isaiah 10; 45; and Jeremiah 29). It was precisely this tension which came to its head when, in John's story, Jesus stood before the Roman governor and declared that, even though he was about to execute him, the power by which he did it had come from God in the first place (John 19:11).

   What does it mean for Christians today that, on the one hand, God wants his world to be governed under the rule of appropriate law and, on the other, that Jesus is already installed as the supreme Lord of heaven and earth?

6. Verses 8-14 show Paul using the idea of fulfilling the law through love. How can love fulfill all of the law?

7. Why does Paul use the image of day in verses 11-14 to explain the behavior that he expects Christians to engage in and the image of night for what they shouldn't do?

8. In verse 13 Paul notes three pairs of activities Christians should avoid. How are bad temper and jealousy just as destructive in a Christian community as drunkenness and sexual immorality?

9. Paul's solution to avoiding the activities of the night is to "put on the Lord Jesus" (v. 14). How are we to do this?

10. In what ways does this entire chapter set a course for the church to live attractive lives in the local community, surrounded as they are by the watching stares of puzzled pagans?

11. Think about your Christian community, your church or a small group. In what ways can your community live in a way that is more attractive to the surrounding culture?

PRAY

Pray through this passage in response to the above question. Pray using the very words of this passage: "love your neighbor," "put off the works of darkness," "put on the armor of light," "put on the Lord Jesus, the Messiah."

NOTE ON ROMANS 13:11

Did Paul think the world was coming to an end soon? Doesn't he say in verse 11 that salvation is about to burst upon the world? And if he was wrong about that, might he not have been wrong about the new day dawning at all?

In 1 Thessalonians 2 Paul says that the Christians in Thessalonica mustn't be worried if they get a letter saying the Day of the Lord had arrived. That Day couldn't have involved the end of the world or the Thessalonians would have noticed! Clearly Paul seems to have thought of great crises that were coming *within* history, not simply to end it. Also, what Paul has said about the coming new world in Romans 8:18-27 indicates clearly enough that the new world will be the liberation of the present world, not its abolition.

The point Paul is making is not that the final day of salvation is bound to happen within a *short* time, but that it might come at *any* time. This was because the event which prepared the way for the final day of salvation, the resurrection of Jesus, had already happened. God's new world had been launched. The sun was already rising, and it was time to get up.

THE WAY OF
LOVE AND PEACE

Romans 14:1-23

After a heavy snowfall a father offered his son the chance to earn some extra pocket money by shoveling a path to the front gate. The son, eager for his pay, put on his boots and coat, grabbed the shovel and began work. Shovelfuls of snow flew this way and that. He kept his head down, concentrating on making a good, complete job of it. Eventually he stood up, drew breath and looked with satisfaction down the length of the path. His father came out. "Well done," he said. "Come and have a cup of cocoa and get your pay."

But as they were going inside they heard a voice. "Then will you come and clear away all the extra snow you've put on *my* path?" It was the next-door neighbor, standing at his door, looking not only at his snowy front garden, but at all the snow that had been shoveled so energetically off their path and onto his. Father and son looked at each other. The neighbor wasn't cross, indeed he was amused, but clearly something had to be done. "I think that looks like a two-man job," said his father.

Paul's supreme concern in chapter 14 is the danger of so clearing your own path that you end up making it impossible for your neighbors to walk down theirs. It is all too easy, in sorting out our own lives and finding our own way forward as Christians, to make things harder, not easier for those around us.

OPEN

What are some of the differences of opinions within your Christian community, church or small group?

STUDY

1. *Read Romans 14:1-23.* If we are correct in assuming that Paul was writing Romans not long after the Jews were allowed to return to Rome in A.D. 54, Jewish Christians would have been returning to a church filled with Gentile believers who had come from pagan backgrounds.

   In a city like Rome, many animals were slaughtered as sacrifices in pagan temples and then served up in an adjoining eating establishment or offered for sale in the open market. There it would likely be impossible to know which meat had been part of a pagan sacrifice and which had not. No devout Jew would dream of eating meat that had been. Many Gentile Christians too, having been regular attenders at pagan temples before their conversion, avoided anything that reminded them of the lifestyle that went with their former beliefs.

   Who does Paul consider to be the "weak in faith" and, by implication, the "strong in faith"?

2. What attitude are the two groups to have toward each other?

3. How is Paul attempting to break down barriers between ethnic groups in verses 1-6?

4. Over what issues in today's church are we in danger of judging one another because of things that Paul would declare to be unimportant?

5. Where are we prone to build walls of division on cultural or ethnic lines where Paul would gently but firmly insist that we are all serving the same master?

6. What is Paul getting at in verses 7-9?

7. How can condemnation become a consequence of differing opinions (vv. 7-12)?

8. What is the overriding perspective that the Christians in Rome need to learn in dealing with differences with each other?

9. How can we as believers know on which issues we can live with differences of opinion and which we cannot?

10. Paul says in verse 14 that nothing is unclean in itself, but how does he say something can become "unclean" (vv. 13-23)?

11. Paul is concerned that Jewish Christians, returning to Rome, may see Gentile Christians doing things that, from their point of view, were associated with paganism, and they may look on in horror. They might even conclude that they had made an awful mistake, call down curses on this new movement (v. 16) and give up the faith altogether.

    How might behaving in accordance with love prevent this from happening?

12. In what specific ways does the church today reverse verse 17 and make God's kingdom about "food and drink" rather than about justice, peace and joy?

13. What would help us turn our focus to justice, peace and joy?

PRAY

Sit in silence and ask God to show you how you have piled snow on another person's path. Spend a few minutes praying silent prayers of confession over the things that God brings to mind.

COMING TO
ROME AT LAST

Romans 15:1-24

Sometimes people come to the letter to the Romans with particular questions to which they find the answers in the earlier chapters and then overlook the rest of the book. That would be like listening to the first ten minutes of a magnificent symphony and then, having heard a favorite tune, walking out of the concert.

Paul will conclude shortly with some personal comments at the end of Romans 15 and in Romans 16. But here in the first part of Romans 15, Paul ends where he began in Romans 1. Jesus, the son of David who is also the son of God, Jesus who has risen from the dead, Jesus is now the Lord of the whole world. In Romans 1 he said that announcing this good news of Jesus was his great calling. Here at the end he again recalls his glorious passion.

OPEN

What is a dream you have about your life and how you would like to serve God?

STUDY

1. *Read Romans 15:1-24.* In verses 1-6, Paul continues his line of thought from chapter 14 about the "strong" and the "weak." In this context, how does Paul exhort us to follow the example of Christ?

2. Because he draws on a passage from the Old Testament (Psalm 69:9), Paul briefly discusses his view of the role of Scripture. What is that role?

3. The whole point of the discussion from Romans 14:1 onward has been to address the situation of how Christians are to live alongside other Christians who do *not* think like them, and how they must not try to force others into the position they themselves have taken up. How is Paul's argument different now in verses 5-6?

4. What do the Old Testament references in verses 7-13 have in common? (If you are interested they are found in Psalm 18:49, Deuteronomy 32:43; Psalm 117:1; and Isaiah 11:10.)

5. What do these passages reveal again about God's ultimate purposes in the world that Paul has been emphasizing throughout the letter to the Romans?

6. How do these truths, especially as seen in verse 7, help us to mutually welcome Christians from different backgrounds, values, cultures and ethnicities?

7. Paul moves in verses 14-24 to consider his longing to visit the Roman church and his calling as an apostle. How does Paul see himself as an Old Testament "priest" in the ministry of the gospel?

8. What is Paul's special calling and vocation?

9. The situation in Rome was a bit complicated for Paul. There were Jewish Christians who had left Rome some years previously and had now returned. Some of them had been members of churches Paul had founded and had actually worked alongside Paul as trusted friends and colleagues. Some of them, though, were native Roman Christians who had embraced the faith when it had been previously proclaimed by others, perhaps even Peter.

   What seems to be Paul's concern in coming to visit and minister in Rome (vv. 14-24)?

10. There is no evidence that Paul ever got to Spain. But his desire to go there and, perhaps, establish a new "home base" was one of the reasons he wrote the letter to the Romans. Paul may not have gotten to Spain, but what mattered then, and has mattered enormously in

the whole history of the church, is that, as part of his plan to go to Spain, he wrote Romans.

What lesson is there for us in the fact that Paul wrote Romans in preparation for a dream that he may never have realized?

PRAY

Pray that you would see the small things that God is accomplishing for his purposes as you pursue a dream he has placed in your heart.

FAMILY AND FRIENDS

Romans 15:25—16:27

In the final chapters of Romans Paul speaks about a journey he must make and tasks he must complete before he can come to Rome to visit the believers there. He has a clear sense of vocation to come to Rome, but there are major battles up ahead before he can get there. First, he must go the opposite direction—to Jerusalem, to the church in Judaea.

The church in Judaea may have been poor due to the fact that, in their first flush of enthusiasm for the gospel, they had done what some other renewal movements of their day had done. They had pooled their property, selling farms and fields and putting the money into common possessions. But now, following a famine, and no doubt facing hostility from their own fellow Judaeans who rejected the gospel and resented their allegiance to it, they were in dire need.

A second issue in Judaea that Paul faced was that from Judaea had come settled and sustained Christian opposition to Paul and his gospel which had followed him from the early days in Galatia. How easy it would have been at this point for Paul to turn his back on them and work with others. But it is precisely these people, the source of the opposition to some of his work, for whom Paul is now undertaking a difficult and dangerous mission.

Romans 15 and 16 look ahead to Paul's future, enlist the help of the Roman believers and highlight his dear friends.

OPEN

Who are some of the people who have had the most influence on your spiritual journey?

STUDY

1. *Read Romans 15:25-33.* How does the collection for the poor Christians of Jerusalem reinforce what Paul has been saying throughout Romans about the church?

2. What does it mean for Jewish Christians to be family with Gentiles and for Gentile believers to be family with the Jewish believers?

3. Why is it so crucial for Paul to enlist the prayers of the Roman church for the journey ahead of him?

4. *Read Romans 16:1-27.* What observations do you make from the list of greetings in verses 1-16?

5. What do you notice about the house churches in Rome and their leadership?

6. Phoebe is the letter-bearer, entrusted with the fullest and most remarkable letter of Paul. What can be learned about Phoebe from verses 1-2?

7. The "holy kiss" (v. 16) became a key feature of Christian liturgy very early on, but it was not meant to replace normal expressions of affection; in many parts of the Middle East and elsewhere a kiss on both cheeks is a normal greeting between men as well as women. How does even this simple gesture reinforce the main themes Paul has written about throughout Romans regarding the church?

8. What is the main point that Paul wants the church in Rome to understand in verses 17-20?

9. How can we use Paul's guidance here to discern "false teaching" in the church today?

10. Paul sends greetings in verses 21-23 from friends of his to the Roman believers. How might these greetings have affected the Roman church?

11. What main themes from the whole letter, reviewed in verses 25-27, have stayed in your mind and heart the most?

12. What has changed in your life since studying the letter to the Romans?

PRAY

Spend time praying through verses 25-27. Praise God for all he has done. Praise God for the specific ways in which he has changed people through this study.

GUIDELINES FOR LEADERS

My grace is sufficient for you.
(2 Corinthians 12:9)

If leading a small group is something new for you, don't worry. These sessions are designed to flow naturally and be led easily. You may even find that the studies seem to lead themselves!

This study guide is flexible. You can use it with a variety of groups—students, professionals, coworkers, friends, neighborhood or church groups. Each study takes forty-five to sixty minutes in a group setting.

You don't need to be an expert on the Bible or a trained teacher to lead a small group. These guides are designed to facilitate a group's discussion, not a leader's presentation. Guiding group members to discover together what the Bible has to say and to listen together for God's guidance will help them remember much more than a lecture would.

There are some important facts to know about group dynamics and encouraging discussion. The suggestions listed below should equip you to effectively and enjoyably fulfill your role as leader.

PREPARING FOR THE STUDY

1. Ask God to help you understand and apply the passage in your own life. Unless this happens, you will not be prepared to lead others. Pray too for the various members of the group. Ask God to open

your hearts to the message of his Word and motivate you to action.

2. Read the introduction to the entire guide to get an overview of the topics that will be explored.

3. As you begin each study, read and reread the assigned Bible passage to familiarize yourself with it. This study guide is based on the For Everyone series on the New Testament (published by SPCK and Westminster John Knox). It will help you and the group if you have on hand a copy of the companion volume from the For Everyone series both for the translation of the passage found there and for further insight into the passage.

4. Carefully work through each question in the study. Spend time in meditation and reflection as you consider how to respond.

5. Write your thoughts and responses in the space provided in the study guide. This will help you to express your understanding of the passage clearly.

6. It may help to have a Bible dictionary handy. Use it to look up any unfamiliar words, names or places. The glossary at the end of each New Testament for Everyone commentary may likewise be helpful for keeping discussion moving.

7. Reflect seriously on how you need to apply the Scripture to your life. Remember that the group members will follow your lead in responding to the studies. They will not go any deeper than you do.

LEADING THE STUDY

1. At the beginning of your first time together, explain that these studies are meant to be discussions, not lectures. Encourage the members of the group to participate. However, do not put pressure on those who may be hesitant to speak—especially during the first few sessions.

2. Be sure that everyone in your group has a study guide. Encourage the group to prepare beforehand for each discussion by reading the introduction to the guide and by working through the questions in each study.

3. Begin each study on time. Open with prayer, asking God to help the group to understand and apply the passage.

4. Have a group member read aloud the introduction at the beginning of the discussion.

5. Discuss the "Open" question before the Bible passage is read. The "Open" question introduces the theme of the study and helps group members to begin to open up, and can reveal where our thoughts and feelings need to be transformed by Scripture. Reading the passage first will tend to color the honest reactions people would otherwise give—because they are, of course, supposed to think the way the Bible does. Encourage as many members as possible to respond to the "Open" question, and be ready to get the discussion going with your own response.

6. Have a group member read aloud the passage to be studied as indicated in the guide.

7. The study questions are designed to be read aloud just as they are written. You may, however, prefer to express them in your own words.

   There may be times when it is appropriate to deviate from the study guide. For example, a question may have already been answered. If so, move on to the next question. Or someone may raise an important question not covered in the guide. Take time to discuss it, but try to keep the group from going off on tangents.

8. Avoid answering your own questions. An eager group quickly becomes passive and silent if members think the leader will do most of the talking. If necessary repeat or rephrase the question until it is clearly understood, or refer to the commentary woven into the guide to clarify the context or meaning.

9. Don't be afraid of silence in response to the discussion questions. People may need time to think about the question before formulating their answers.

10. Don't be content with just one answer. Ask, "What do the rest of you think?" or "Anything else?" until several people have given answers to the question.

11. Try to be affirming whenever possible. Affirm participation. Never reject an answer; if it is clearly off-base, ask, "Which verse led you to that conclusion?" or again, "What do the rest of you think?"

12. Don't expect every answer to be addressed to you, even though this will probably happen at first. As group members become more at ease, they will begin to truly interact with each other. This is one sign of healthy discussion.

13. Don't be afraid of controversy. It can be very stimulating. If you don't resolve an issue completely, don't be frustrated. Explain that the group will move on and God may enlighten all of you in later sessions.

14. Periodically summarize what the group has said about the passage. This helps to draw together the various ideas mentioned and gives continuity to the study. But don't preach.

15. Conclude your time together with the prayer suggestion at the end of the study, adapting it to your group's particular needs as appropriate. Ask for God's help in following through on the applications you've identified.

16. End on time.

Many more suggestions and helps for studying a passage or guiding discussion can be found in *How to Lead a LifeGuide Bible Study* and *The Big Book on Small Groups* (both from InterVarsity Press/USA).

Other InterVarsity Press Resources from N. T. Wright

The Challenge of Jesus
N. T. Wright offers clarity and a full accounting of the facts of the life and teachings of Jesus, revealing how the Son of God was also solidly planted in first-century Palestine. *978-0-8308-2200-3, 202 pages, hardcover*

Resurrection
This 50-minute DVD confronts the most startling claim of Christianity—that Jesus rose from the dead. Shot on location in Israel, Greece and England, N. T. Wright presents the political, historical and theological issues of Jesus' day and today regarding this claim. Wright brings clarity and insight to one of the most profound mysteries in human history. Study guide included.
978-0-8308-3435-8, DVD

Evil and the Justice of God
N. T. Wright explores all aspects of evil and how it presents itself in society today. Fully grounded in the story of the Old and New Testaments, this presentation is provocative and hopeful; a fascinating analysis of and response to the fundamental question of evil and justice that faces believers.
978-0-8308-3398-6, 176 pages, hardcover

Evil
Filmed in Israel, South Africa and England, this 50-minute DVD confronts some of the major "evil" issues of our time—from tsunamis to AIDS—and puts them under the biblical spotlight. N. T. Wright says there is a solution to the problem of evil, if only we have the honesty and courage to name it and understand it for what it is. Study guide included. *978-0-8308-3434-1, DVD*

Justification: God's Plan and Paul's Vision
In this comprehensive account and defense of the crucial doctrine of justification, Wright also responds to critics who have challenged what has come to be called the new perspective. Ultimately, he provides a chance for those in the middle of and on both sides of the debate to interact directly with his views and form their own conclusions. *978-0-8308-3863-9, 279 pages, hardcover*

Colossians and Philemon
In Colossians, Paul presents Christ as "the firstborn over all creation," and appeals to his readers to seek a maturity found only Christ. In Philemon, Paul appeals to a fellow believer to receive a runaway slave in love and forgiveness. In this volume N. T. Wright offers comment on both of these important books.
978-0-8308-4242-1, 199 pages, paperback